On the Trail of the Presidents

An Historical Guide

to

Burial Sites

and

Monuments

By Jack B. Jones & Joy E. Jones

Dedicated to our children and grandchildren
in the hope they will each be able to take this
historical journey in search of the Presidents.

Graphics by Erick

Table of Contents

	page			page
1. George Washington	1	20. James A. Garfield	49
2. John Adams	5	21. Chester A. Arthur	51
3. Thomas Jefferson	9	22. Grover Cleveland	53
4. James Madison	13	23. Benjamin Harrison	55
5. James Monroe	15	24. Grover Cleveland	53
6. John Quincy Adams	17	25. William McKinley	57
7. Andrew Jackson	19	26. Theodore Roosevelt	59
8. Martin Van Buren	21	27. William H. Taft	61
9. William Harrison	23	28. Woodrow Wilson	63
10. John Tyler	25	29. Warren G. Harding	67
11. James K. Polk	27	30. Calvin Coolidge	69
12. Zachary Taylor	29	31. Herbert Hoover	71
13. Millard Fillmore	31	32. Franklin D. Roosevelt	73
14. Franklin Pierce	33	33. Harry S. Truman	77
15. James Buchanan	35	34. Dwight D. Eisenhower	79
16. Abraham Lincoln	37	35. John F. Kennedy	81
17. Andrew Johnson	41	36. Lyndon B. Johnson	83
18. Ulysses S. Grant	43	37. Richard M. Nixon	85
19. Rutherford B. Hayes	47		

Introduction

Why this book? Many people have asked that question of the authors during all phases of preparation and production. The answer has several facets ranging from a long-standing desire to provide travelers with a tour guide which will entertain and instruct the reader as he/she seeks the resting places of our presidents throughout our nation, to a purpose (if any is needed) for exploring this vibrant, exciting, historical nation.

The principal underlying motivation however, is based on the fact that no matter how long or short a president served his country, that his contribution to the development and hence greatness of our nation is due to his service at that time. Therefore, each president should be honored, respected, and appreciated for his efforts on our behalf, no matter what greatness or affliction is ascribed to him.

While writing this history and guide to the burial places of the presidents several impressions were gained and incorporated in the text. A major revelation was that not all presidents were created equal nor buried the same. Some of our reputed greatest presidents are buried in the most humble and unpretentious graves (e.g. Madison, Wilson, Adams), while some of the lesser known or revered presidents (e.g. Harding, Garfield, Andrew Johnson, W. Harrison) are buried in large, well-maintained monuments.

The circumstance of burial varies widely from president to president. Therefore, some are buried in community city cemeteries, some in churches, some at their ancestral homes, some in National cemeteries, while a few are buried in sites especially created for the tomb.

Some presidents are buried in a sarcophagus above ground, some under their monument, some in their monument, some beside their monument, and some in traditional graves with a headstone. None were cremated. Maintenance of graves or tombs varies greatly from burial site to burial site and this condition is commented on in the text.

Featured in the text are state maps with flagged locations of the presidential burial sites and written directions for finding them. (A word of caution, be sure to double-check directions whenever possible. It was found on occasion that roads were eliminated, renamed, or changed to one-way streets between visits to tombs which had been visited a few years earlier.)

Each entry contains some basic common biographical information such as birthdate, date of death, etc. as well as some lesser known but interesting facts about each president. For instance, no president as yet, has died in the month of May and of the 41 presidents, over half (21) have served in the Armed Forces of the United States, including the militia. It is interesting to note that of those presidents serving in the armed services, John Kennedy was the first Navy president and that six of the last eight presidents to serve were also Navy Veterans. President Reagan served with the Army during World War II. President Clinton had no military service nor did six other presidents in this century: Taft, Wilson, Harding, Coolidge, Hoover, or Franklin Roosevelt. None the less, as Commander in Chief of all military forces, most of our presidents have been called upon to commit the armed forces of our nation into some form of action during their tenure as president and are truly veterans and honored as such.

It is the authors' hope that the reader will be able to visit at least one if not all the current burial sights and experience the historical significance of each president's contribution to our present greatness and the closeness of each president's humanness.

To Use This Guide

The Guide to Presidential Interment Sites is written in the order in which our presidents served, beginning with George Washington and ending with Richard M. Nixon.

Suggested tour guides are provided in the appendices which group burial sites predicated on geographical areas more easily undertaken. The tours are based on a leisurely driving pace (car speed 50 mph), length of time at burial site (2 hours) and average time between sites (8 hours). With time taken for meals, etc., one should be able to reach a site each day. Time expended for side-trips and vacationing was not considered in the calculations.

If one were to visit every Presidential Interment Site in one complete tour, the estimated time based on the variables above would require approximately 45 days depending of course on point of departure and return.

Note: Most sites are accessible 365 days a year. Those maintained by National Park Service are closed on Christmas Day and/or New Year's Day.

Acknowledgments

Our heartfelt thanks to:
Jean & Erland Dettloff
Dick & Agnes Jones
Dixie & Bob Hoagland
Diane & Bob Levison
Marysue & Bob Chapman
Jennifer & Erick Wand
for hours of proofreading and encouragement
and to the many helpful Park Service people on our journey who helped so much in our research.

Presidential Burial Sites by State

Virginia - seven

George Washington: Mt. Vernon
Thomas Jefferson: Charlottesville
James Madison: Montpelier Station
John Tyler: Richmond
John Kennedy: Arlington
William Howard Taft: Arlington
James Monroe: Richmond

New York - six

Martin Van Buren: Kinderhook
Ulysses S. Grant: New York City
Franklin Delano Roosevelt: Hyde Park
Millard Fillmore: Buffalo
Theodore Roosevelt: Oyster Bay
Chester Arthur: Albany

Ohio - five

Wm. H. Harrison: North Bend
James A. Garfield: Cleveland
Warren G. Harding: Marion
Rutherford B. Hayes: Fremont
William McKinley: Canton

Tennessee - three

Andrew Jackson: Nashville
James Knox Polk: Nashville
Andrew Johnson: Greeneville

Massachusetts - two

John Adams: Quincy
John Quincy Adams: Quincy

One site each state:

Zachary Taylor: Louisville, KY
Lyndon Johnson: Stonewall, TX
Woodrow Wilson: Washington, D.C.
Dwight D. Eisenhower: Abilene, KS
Abraham Lincoln: Springfield, IL
Calvin Coolidge: Plymouth, VT
Herbert Hoover: West Branch, IA

Benjamin Harrison: Indianapolis, IN
Harry S. Truman: Independence, MO
James Buchanan: Lancaster, PA
Franklin Pierce: Concord, NH
Grover Cleveland: Princeton, NJ
Richard M. Nixon: Yorba Linda, CA

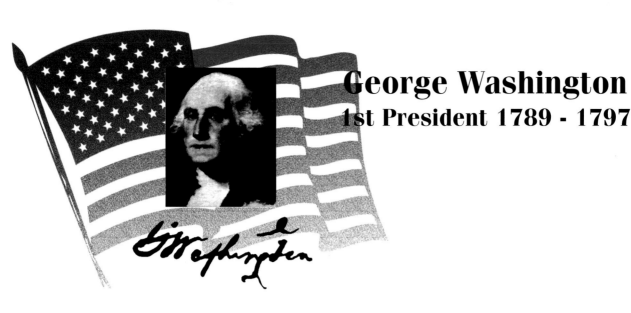

George Washington
1st President 1789 - 1797

Born: Wakefield (Westmoreland County), Virginia
          February 22, 1732

Died: Mount Vernon, Virginia
          December 14, 1799

Age at Death: 67

Place of Burial: Mt. Vernon

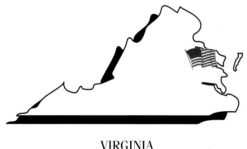

VIRGINIA

Mount Vernon, Virginia

Commonly called "The Father of our Country," George Washington began the administration of the presidency with no model; no preconceptions; no job description. His primary concern was that no matter what he did, he must exercise care because he realized that he was setting a precedent to be followed by others.

George Washington was raised on his father's farm, attending school on and off until he was fifteen years of age. He was an excellent horseman and experienced hunter. He became a surveyor at age fifteen and surveyed the Shenandoah Valley. At age twenty-one he began his military career. He served at one time with the British Army during the French and Indian Wars as General Braddock's aide, the only president ever to serve with the British Army. After approximately six years of service he left the military to return to farming at Mount Vernon. After the Battle of Concord and Lexington in April 1775, he was appointed Commander in Chief of all American forces by the Continental Congress. Although he won fewer battles than the British, he stayed in the field which denied the British total victory. Later at Yorktown, he soundly defeated the British, who were then willing to sue for peace.

After the war, Washington went to Philadelphia for the Continental Congress where he was elected chairman. Subsequently he was elected president. He was sworn in as President on April 30, 1789.

Elected to a second term in 1792, he gave the shortest inaugural speech of any president: 135 words. After serving two terms, he retired to his farm in 1797.

Two years later, after riding around his farm, Washington was caught in a snowstorm and the resulting illness caused pneumonia. For two days, doctors reportedly "bled" him, which was a common practice at that time, but he died shortly thereafter. He died at his home, Mt. Vernon at the age of 67.

Location:	Mt. Vernon is located at the southernmost end of the Mt. Vernon Memorial Highway (State Hwy. 233) approximately eight miles south of Alexandria, Virginia and 15 miles south from Washington, D. C.
Burial Facts:	George Washington was buried in the vault of the family cemetery at Mt. Vernon in 1799. Though he had selected the present site for his burial, the vault was not built until 1831 at which time his remains were moved to the vault where he was placed in his marble sarcophagus. When he died he left his wife, Martha and her two children by a previous marriage. Martha is also buried at Mt. Vernon with President Washington.
Graveside Condition:	Excellent. The grounds of Mt. Vernon and the tomb are well-maintained by the Mount Vernon Ladies' Association of the Union, a nonprofit organization which receives no support from Federal or State government.
Directions:	From Alexandria/Washington D. C. area, take Virginia State Highway 233 South. This highway is also called the Mount Vernon Memorial Highway. Travel south approximately eight miles from Alexandria, Virginia until the road terminates at Mt. Vernon. A large parking area at that location is provided free of charge. It is approximately one-half mile to the grave site on the grounds of Mount Vernon Estate.

John Adams
2nd President 1797-1801

Born:	Braintree (Quincy), Massachusetts October 30, 1735
Died:	Quincy, Massachusetts July 4, 1826
Age at Death:	90
Place of Burial:	United First Parish Church (Unitarian) Quincy, Massachusetts

MASSACHUSETTS

United First Parish Church (Unitarian) in Quincy

Shortly before John Adams died he said, "Independence now: independence forever." These words accurately describe Adams the man and Adams the patriot. Raised on a small farm in Braintree, Massachusetts, Adams attended Harvard University and graduated intent on a teaching career, or one in the ministry. After he taught school, he studied law and was admitted to the bar in 1758. When relations with England became strained, he became a strong advocate for independence, opposing the Stamp Act and serving as attorney for those patriots indicted by the British. He participated in the Continental Congress in 1776 and, along with Thomas Jefferson, signed the Declaration of Independence. During the revolution he served as Commissioner to France. He helped negotiate the peace treaty with Britain at war's end and in 1785 was named Ambassador to London.

He was elected Vice President under George Washington, serving two terms. He was reported to have said about the Vice Presidency that "...was the most insignificant office that ever the invention of man contrived or his imagination conceived." He was elected President in

1796. During his presidency relations with France deteriorated and members of his administration, led by Alexander Hamilton advocated war; however Adam's policies averted war with France but resulted in a split in his party and with Hamilton. This split allowed Thomas Jefferson, his vice president to be elected president thus denying Adams a second term. John Adams retired to his home in Quincy, Massachusetts, where he died at age 90 on July 4, 1826. His last words were "Jefferson still survives," but Jefferson had died a few hours earlier on the same day.

Adams was the president born furthest east of all presidents, lived the longest (90 years), was married the longest (54 years to Abigail Adams) and the first president to live in the Executive Mansion (White House), when he moved the capitol from Philadelphia to Washington, D. C.

Location:	Downtown Quincy, Massachusetts, a suburb southeast of Boston, east of Interstate Highway 93 at 1306 Hancock St.
Burial Facts:	John Adams died of "old age" at the age of 90 in Quincy, Massachusetts. Preceded in death by his wife, Abigail (Smith) Adams in 1818, he was first buried along with her in the Hancock Cemetery until 1828 when they were reinterred in the First Parish Church. Today, John Adams, his wife Abigail, his son, John Quincy Adams and John Quincy Adam's wife Louisa, are buried in the vault in the basement of the United First Parish Church (Unitarian).
Graveside Condition:	Excellent. Well preserved and maintained by the United First Parish Church.
Directions:	From downtown Boston, travel south approximately 4 miles on Interstate 93 to Hancock Street Exit (State Highway 3). Proceed approximately two miles on Hancock St. to the church at 1306 Hancock St. Note: The United First Parish Church occupies a small block in the center of Quincy, and parking is scarce.

Thomas Jefferson
3rd President 1801-1809

VIRGINIA

Born: Goochland (now Albemarle) County, Virginia
April 13, 1743 at Shadwell

Died: Charlottesville, Virginia
July 4, 1826 at "Monticello"

Age at Death: 83

Place of Burial: Family cemetery on grounds of Monticello,
Charlottesville, VA

Monticello

If any President could be called a "Renaissance man," Thomas Jefferson was that man: writer, inventor, scientist, architect, musician, philosopher, patriot, politician, leader, governor, president. Jefferson was raised in western Virginia, the frontier of the south. He attended William and Mary College from 1760 - 1762, graduating with a Bachelor of Arts. He read classics in Greek and Latin and played the violin. Although he studied law, he was always interested in science and philosophy. His literary skill and political acumen brought him to the forefront of the revolutionary movement in Virginia and he was elected to the Continental Congress. He drafted the Declaration of Independence. In 1776 he was elected to the Virginia House of Delegates (Burgess) and in 1779 Governor of Virginia. He abdicated when the British invaded in 1781 and retired to his home "Monticello" which he had begun constructing in 1770. His wife Martha Wayles Skelton, whom he married in 1772, died in 1782. In 1783 he was sent to Congress where he helped initiate the decimal system which is the basis for our monetary system today. In 1785 he was minister to France and in 1789 Washington appointed him Secretary of State. He was elected Vice President under John Adams in 1796 and in 1801 became the third President of the United States. He was the first President inaugurated in

Washington D. C. (a city he helped design) and served two terms. He retired to Monticello in 1809 and developed interest in education, founding the University of Virginia. He died at Monticello July 4, 1826.

Location: "Monticello." Jefferson's home and burial site are located approximately 2 miles south-east of Charlottesville on State Highway 53. A parking lot is located on the grounds with a shuttle to the estate.

Burial Facts: Thomas Jefferson died of diarrhea at his home "Monticello" on July 4th, 1826 and is buried in the family cemetery located on the grounds of the estate approximately 500 yards downhill from the rear of the main house.

Graveside Condition: Well maintained and protected, the tomb is within an iron-bar protected plot. The inscription on his tomb reads:
>   Here was buried Thomas Jefferson
>   Author of the Declaration of Independence
>   of the Statute of Virginia for Religious Freedom
>   And father of the University of Virginia.

Directions: From Charlottesville, Virginia, take State Highway 20 South, crossing Interstate 64 to State Highway 53. Follow State Highway 53 approximately 1.5 miles to main parking area.

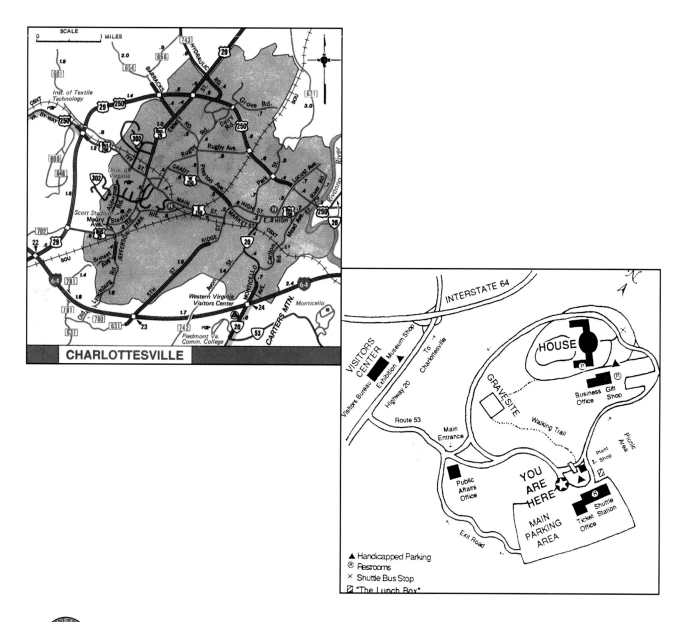

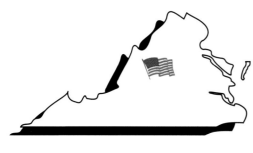

James Madison
4th President 1809 - 1817

Born: Port Conway, Virginia
March 16, 1751

Died: Montpelier, Montpelier Station, VA
June 28, 1836

Age at Death: 85

Place of Burial: Family cemetery near
Montpelier Plantation
Montpelier Station, VA

VIRGINIA

Montpelier Cemetery

One of three presidents born as a British citizen, James Madison, our shortest president at five feet four inches tall, was home-taught until age 18. He attended Princeton University, graduating in 1771 after two years. He studied theology, but decided to pursue a career in politics. He was a member of the Continental Congress and a significant framer of the United States Constitution. He was elected to the House of Representatives in 1789 and led the fight to add the Bill of Rights, the first ten amendments. He was Jefferson's Secretary of State and elected president in 1808. President during the War of 1812, called Madison's War, he was the first and only president to flee the White House for safety because of imminent danger of battle. Madison retired to his estate after leaving the presidency later becoming Rector of the University of Virginia.

Location: 4 miles west of Orange, Virginia, 1 mile off Virginia State Rt. 20. Sign "Madison Grave-yard" on south side of highway. Note: Madison's estate "Montpelier" is located near Montpelier Station, Virginia near Orange, Virginia and not in Montpelier, which is approximately 45 miles east of Montpelier Station.

Burial Facts. James Madison died of natural causes and debility at age 85 in his home "Montpelier," Montpelier Station near Orange, Virginia. He left his wife, Dorothea (Dolley) 1768 - 1849, but had no children. He is buried with his wife and other family members in the family cemetery, approximately 1 mile west of the family home, "Montpelier" in Montpelier Station, Virginia.

Graveside Condition: Poor. Little if any maintenance in evidence. Some vandalism evident with chips broken off the base of the monument.

Directions: Approaching from the east (Richmond) follow Interstate 64 to Charlottesville; turn north on State Highway 20 for 20 miles to cemetery on right side of Highway. (Approximately 1.5 miles southwest of Montpelier Station, Virginia). Traveling from east on I-64 or north on I-81, remain on I-64 through Charlottesville, turning north on State Highway 20 for approximately 20 miles north to cemetery.

James Monroe
5th President 1817 - 1825

Hollywood Cemetery, Richmond, Virginia

Born: Westmoreland County, Virginia
April 28, 1758

Died: New York City, New York
July 4, 1831

Age at Death: 73

Place of Burial: Hollywood Cemetery
Richmond, Virginia

VIRGINIA

Most noted for the "Monroe Doctrine," the cornerstone of today's U.S. foreign policy, James Monroe was the last of the "Revolution" presidents.

Born in Westmoreland County, Virginia near Colonial Beach, Virginia, he was tutored at home, later attending William and Mary College. He left school abruptly to fight in the Revolutionary War, rising to the rank of Major. He fought in several major battles and was wounded at the battle of Trenton.

After the war he studied law with Thomas Jefferson and in 1780 became a member of the Virginia House of Delegates. He served in Congress from 1782 - 1786. In 1790 he was elected to the U.S. Senate. From 1794 - 1796 and again in 1803 he was minister to France where he helped negotiate the Louisiana Purchase. From 1799 - 1802 he was Governor of Virginia. In 1810 - 1811 he served in the Virginia Assembly and was then appointed Secretary of State by James Madison from 1811 - 1817. He was elected President on the Democratic-Republic Ticket in 1816 and reelected in 1820.

He retired to his home "Oak Hill" near Leesburg, Virginia and served as a regent for University of Virginia. Forced to sell his home for financial reasons, he moved to New York to live with his daughter where he died of debility (old age) at 73. Of the five presidents (Washington, John Adams, Thomas Jefferson, James Madison and Monroe) who were part of the Revolution, three of these presidents, Jefferson, Adams, and Monroe died on the Fourth of July. Monroe was preceded in death by his wife, Elizabeth Kortright Monroe on September 23, 1830.

Location:	James Monroe is buried on the "Presidents" Hill in Hollywood Cemetery near John Tyler and Jefferson Davis (President of the Confederacy): 412 South Cherry St. Richmond, Virginia.
Burial Facts:	Having died of debility and old age at 73 years, he was first interred in New York City where he died, but was reinterred in Richmond in 1858.
Graveside Condition:	Adequately maintained and protected by Hollywood Cemetery personnel. Monroe's marble sarcophagus is protected by iron cupolas and grates among other grave sites nearby.
Directions:	From downtown Richmond, Virginia, take the "Downtown Expressway" west to Laurel Street. Travel south on Laurel to Albemarle St. Turn right (west) one block to Cherry Street, then right (north) on Cherry to entrance of the cemetery. The Confederate Monument (a large pyramid) will mark the entrance.

John Quincy Adams
6th President 1825 - 1829

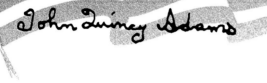

Born: July 11, 1767
Quincy, Massachusetts (Braintree)

Died: February 23, 1848
Washington D. C.

Age at Death: 80

Place of Burial: First Parish Church
Quincy, Massachusetts

MASSACHUSETTS

United First Parish Church

The only son of a United States President to be elected President of the United States, John Quincy Adams attended school in Europe, where his father served in various countries as a diplomat. John Quincy Adams attended Harvard University, graduating in 1787, Phi Beta Kappa. He then studied law and was sent by President Washington as a diplomat to Europe. He was elected to the U. S. Senate, serving from 1803 - 1808. He was Secretary of State under Monroe and helped formulate the Monroe Doctrine. He was elected President in 1824, garnering only 29.8% of the popular vote, and only 31.8% of the electoral vote, making him the first "minority" President. He was the first President to win the election in the House of Representatives because he did not win the majority of votes in the Electoral College. He was defeated by Andrew Jackson in 1828. In 1831 he was elected to the House of Representatives from Massachusetts, where he served with distinction for seventeen years. He helped establish the Smithsonian Institution and was one of the first presidents to be photographed. He had a stroke while at his desk at the House of Representatives and died in the Speakers' Room February 23, 1848. He was the first and only President to die in the Capitol Building.

Location:	Downtown Quincy, Massachusetts, a suburb southeast of Boston, east of Interstate Highway 93 at 1306 Hancock Street.
Burial Facts:	John Quincy Adams died at the age of 80 due to paralysis brought on by a stroke in the House of Representatives in Washington D. C. He is buried in Quincy, Massachusetts in the vault located in the basement of First Parish Church (Unitarian) along with his wife Louisa Catherine Johnson Adams and his father, John (the second President of the United States) and his mother, Abigail Smith Adams.
Graveside Condition:	Excellent. Well-preserved and maintained by personnel of the United First Parish Church.
Directions:	From downtown Boston, travel south approximately four miles on Interstate 93 to Hancock Street Exit (State Highway 3). Proceed approximately two miles on Hancock St. to the church at 1306 Hancock Street. Note: the United First Parish Church occupies a small block in the center of Quincy and parking is limited.

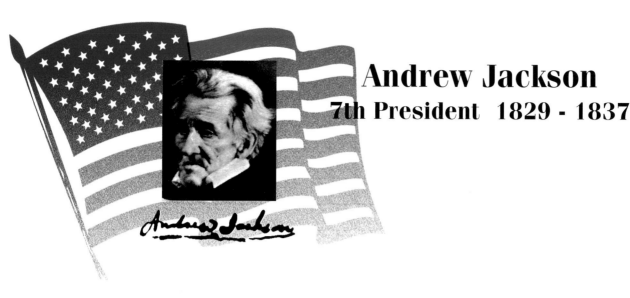

Andrew Jackson
7th President 1829 - 1837

Born: Waxhaw Settlement - South Carolina
March 15, 1767

Died: Nashville, Tennessee
June 8, 1845

Age at Death: 78

Place of Burial: "The Hermitage"
Nashville, Tennessee

The Hermitage

TENNESSEE

One of three presidents to serve in the Revolutionary War and only one of three presidents to serve in the War of 1812, Andrew Jackson served with distinction even though he had no formal military training. He was the first president born in a log cabin and not an aristocrat. He was the youngest of all the presidents to marry, becoming wed to Rachel Robards when he was only eighteen years of age.

Jackson also served in the Tennessee Constitutional Convention in the 1790's, the United States House of Representatives and Senate, and on the Tennessee Supreme Court. During the 1800's, he broke with the Democratic-Republican party of Jefferson and founded the Democratic party and was the first candidate to be nominated by a national political convention. He was a strong-willed man, given to a hot temper, but he proved to be a strong president who left office as highly regarded as when he entered.

Location:	Twelve miles east of Nashville, Tennessee, north off Interstate 40.
Burial Facts:	Andrew Jackson died at the Hermitage, his estate, outside of Nashville, Tennessee on June 8, 1845 of consumption and dropsy at the age of 78. He is buried at that site in the family cemetery along with his wife and other family members.
Gravesite condition:	Excellent. The burial sight along with the grounds of his home are well maintained by the Ladies' Hermitage Association and is a National Historic Landmark.
Directions:	The Hermitage is reached by taking Old Hickory Boulevard exit (Exit 221) north from Interstate 40 East, approximately three miles to Rachel's Lane, turn east to the Hermitage.

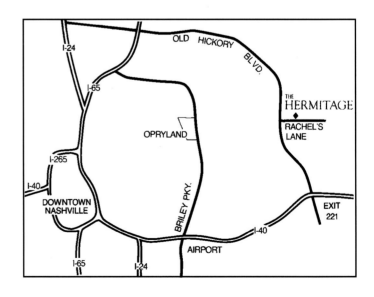

Martin Van Buren
8th President 1837 - 1841

Born: Kinderhook, New York
December 5, 1782

Died: Kinderhook, New York
July 24, 1862

Age at Death: 79

Place of Burial: Kinderhook Cemetery
Kinderhook, New York

NEW YORK

Kinderhook Community Cemetery, Kinderhook, N.Y.

Martin Van Buren was the first president to be born an American citizen. He also was the only president to witness eight presidents to succeed him. Born and raised in Kinderhook, New York, he began studying law at age fourteen and became an attorney at twenty-one. He became Surrogate of Columbia County, New York, State Senator, and then New York Attorney General. He was elected to the United States Senate in 1821 and reelected in 1827. He was Governor of New York from 1828 to 1829. Van Buren was a close friend of Andrew Jackson and served as his Secretary of State and then Vice President during Jackson's second term. He was a consummate politician, known as the "Little Magician," creating a political machine in New York which was inherent to his election. He was the first president elected through use of a political "machine."

Location:	Kinderhook Community Cemetery, Kinderhook, New York is on State Highway 9, 24 miles south of Albany, New York on the east side of the Hudson River.
Burial Facts:	He died of asthma at the age of 79 and is buried with his wife, Hannah Hoes, in the Kinderhook Community Cemetery, Kinderhook, New York.
Graveside Condition:	Average care commensurate with other gravesites in the Community Cemetery. No special protection or precautions against vandalism. Poorly serviced.
Directions:	From Albany, New York, cross the Hudson River and travel south on State Highway 9 for approximately 24 miles to Kinderhook, New York. Cemetery is located off Highway 9 approximately 1.5 miles west of town.

William Henry Harrison
9th President 1841 - 1841

Born: Berkeley Plantation, Charles City County, VA.
February 9, 1773

Died: Washington D. C.
April 4, 1841

Age at Death: 68

Place of Burial: North Bend, Ohio.

OHIO

William Henry Harrison State Park
North Bend, Ohio (Mt. Nebo)

     Born on his father's plantation in Charles City County, Virginia, Harrison attended Hampden-Sydney College, Virginia, where he studied Greek, Latin, and medicine. He served in the U. S. Army from 1791 to 1798. In 1800, he became the Governor of Indiana Territory. In 1811 he again donned the uniform to lead troops against the Indians at the Battle of Tippecanoe. His victory in this battle earned the sobriquet of Old Tippecanoe. He was appointed Major General of the Kentucky Militia in 1812 and served in the U. S. Army from 1812 to 1814 in the War of 1812. His political offices included Secretary of the Northwest Territory, U. S. Representative from Indiana, Governor of Indiana Territory, Ohio State Senator, United States Senator, and Minister to Columbia. He was the first Whig party president and elected as the ninth president, taking office on March 4, 1841. He served for one month, dying on April 4, 1841. Harrison, whose father signed the Declaration of Independence, is noted for having given the longest inaugural speech on record, lasting one hour and forty-five minutes, and containing 8,445 words.

Location:	17 miles southwest of Cincinnati, Ohio on U. S. Highway 50, Loop Avenue, south of Harrison Avenue, North Bend, Ohio.
Burial Facts:	Harrison was the first president to die in office, also the first to die in the White House and lie in state at the White House. He served the shortest time of any president (one month). Dying at the age of 68 from pleuresy and pneumonia, contracted from exposure during his inauguration when subjected to rain and cold. Harrison is buried with his wife, Anna Symmes at William Henry Harrison State Park.
Graveside Condition:	Fair maintenance. Poor protection. The monument sits atop Mt. Nebo in Wm. Henry Harrison State Park in North Bend, Ohio. There are some signs of graffiti.
Directions:	From Cincinnati, travel west on River Road (U. S. Highway 50) approximately 16 miles to North Bend, Ohio. Take Brower Road off Hwy. 50 (River Road). Note: Brower runs parallel to Highway 50. In North Bend, turn right on Miami Ave. for approximately 3/4 mile. Then turn left on Brower Cliff Rd., cross over the overpass and the tomb will be on the right. A small parking lot is at the bottom of the grounds with stairs leading to the tomb.

John Tyler
10th President 1841 - 1845

Born: Charles City County, Virginia
March 29, 1790

Died: Richmond, VA
January 18, 1862

Age at Death: 71

Place of Burial: Hollywood Cemetery
Richmond, VA

VIRGINIA

Hollywood Cemetery

Born on the Greenway Estate in Charles City County, Virginia, John Tyler was sent to William and Mary College in 1802 by his father. He graduated at the age of seventeen and studied law, under his father, being admitted to the Virginia Bar in 1809. He became interested in politics and served as a member of the Virginia House of Delegates, U. S. Representative from Virginia, Governor of Virginia, U. S. Senator, and Vice President under William Henry Harrison. He served as a captain in the military in the latter part of the War of 1812. The second Whig President, he assumed the presidency upon the death of William Henry Harrison and served from April 4, 1841 to March 4, 1845. After retiring from the presidency, he was elected to the Confederate States of America House of Representatives, but died before taking office. He was married to Letitia Christian, who died in the White House in 1842. He then married his second wife, Julia Gardiner, who is buried with him in Hollywood Cemetery. Tyler had fifteen children, eight by his first wife, and seven by his second. Known as the president without a party, because he was thrown out by the Whig party and the Democrats would not have him, he held a different distinction of being the first to marry while in office and the first vice president to ascend to the presidency due to the death of a president.

Location: John Tyler is buried on "Presidents Hill" in Hollywood Cemetery in close proximity to James Monroe and Jefferson Davis (President of the Confederacy), 412 So. Cherry St., Richmond, Virginia.

Burial Facts: Tyler died at the age of 71 due to bilious fever. Despite his support and involvement with the Confederacy, Congress dedicated a monument to Tyler in Hollywood Cemetery.

Graveside Condition: Adequately maintained and protected by Hollywood Cemetery personnel.

Directions: From downtown Richmond, Virginia, take the "Downtown Expressway" west to Laurel Street. Travel South on Laurel to Albemarle St. Turn right (west) one block to Cherry Street, then right (north) on Cherry to entrance of the cemetery. The Confederate Monument (a large pyramid) will mark the entrance.

James Knox Polk
11th President 1845 - 1849

Born: Mecklenburg County, North Carolina
November 2, 1795

Died: Nashville, Tennessee
June 15, 1849

Age at Death: 53

Place of Burial: State Capitol Grounds
Nashville, Tennessee

TENNESSEE

Grounds, Tennessee State Capitol

Born on a farm in North Carolina, James Knox Polk attended private schools as a young-ster. He attended the University of North Carolina, where he received his bachelor's degree. He then studied law in Tennessee and was admitted to the bar. He entered politics, becoming the first professional politician to become president, serving in the Tennessee Legislature as Gov-ernor, and U.S. House of Representatives where he rose to be Speaker of the House. He was the first and only House Speaker to become President. He was also the first "dark horse" candidate in American politics. In 1844 at the Democratic Convention, most thought that Martin Van Buren would get the nomination, however Van Buren could garner only half of the nominating votes and could not get the two-thirds required to win. Andrew Jackson came out for Polk and the convention agreed on Polk as a compromise candidate, making him the first "dark horse" candidate. During his administration, he opened the Oregon Trail and engaged in war with Mexico, acquiring, as a result, California, Nevada, Utah, Arizona, and New Mexico. Other no-table accomplishments during his presidency were the opening of the United States Naval Acad-emy, the laying of the cornerstone of the Washington Monument on July 4, 1848, and the install-ment of gas lights in the White House. President Polk refused to run for a second term, making him the first to have this distinction.

Location:	Capitol Grounds of the Tennessee State Capitol, 6th and Charlotte Ave., Nashville, Tennessee.
Burial Facts:	Polk died of cholera and diarrhea at age 53, and is buried with his wife, Sara Childress, on the grounds of the state capitol in Nashville.
Graveside Condition:	Good condition. Well cared for and maintained by State of Tennessee. Exposed, but protected by Capitol Police.
Directions:	U. S. Interstate Highways 40, 65, 24, and 265 all converge on downtown Nashville. From Interstate 65, take the James Robertson Parkway west to 3rd St. Turn left (south) to Charlotte Ave., then right (west) on Charlotte Ave. to 7th Ave. Turn right (north) on 7th Ave. which will loop up the hill around the Capitol building to a parking lot.

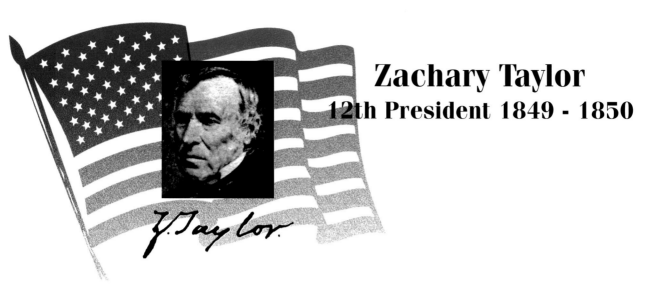

Zachary Taylor
12th President 1849 - 1850

Born:	"Montebello," Orange County, Virginia November 24, 1784
Died:	Washington D.C. July 9, 1850
Age at Death:	65
Place of Burial:	Zachary Taylor National Cemetery, Louisville, Kentucky

Zachary Taylor National Cemetery

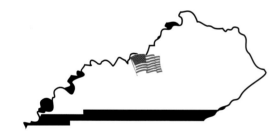

KENTUCKY

A second cousin of James Madison, Zachary Taylor also lived in rural Virginia, was raised on a farm and received tutoring at home. At age twenty-two, he joined the army and fought in the Indian campaigns and the war of 1812. Later he fought both the Blackhawk War and the Seminole Indian War in Florida, where he was promoted to the rank of general. At the outset of the war with Mexico, he was placed in command of an army where he gained national fame at the battle of Buena Vista when his army defeated a Mexican army four times as large as his. It was while he commanded troops that he gained the sobriquet of "Old Rough and Ready." Nominated for president by the Whig Party, he won election primarily because of his war record, having never served in public office or having been a politician. It was due to this lack of political experience that Taylor was not highly regarded for his conduct of the presidency and was disliked by many Americans. He was the second president to die in office in the White House.

Location:	4701 Brownsborro Road. 6 miles east of Louisville, Kentucky on U.S. Highway 42.
Burial Facts:	Taylor is buried with his wife, Margaret Smith, in a small mausoleum at Zachary Taylor National Cemetery, Louisville, Kentucky. He died of coronary thrombosis at age 65. On July 15, 1991, Taylor's body was exhumed for 4 hours to check for evidence of arsenic poisoning. Some historians had alleged that his death was an assassination because of the intense dislike for him. The examination of the body found no unusual levels of arsenic; therefore no case for poisoning. The original family vault was used for the first burial in the 1800s. A second vault was built in 1926, and Taylor's body was placed here, where it remains today. The first vault is approximately 50 yards to the rear of the new mausoleum.
Graveside Condition:	Well cared for, maintained and protected by National Cemetery personnel.
Directions:	From downtown Louisville take U.S. Highway 42 (Brownsborro Rd.) approximately 6 miles east. The entrance is on the north side of the highway.

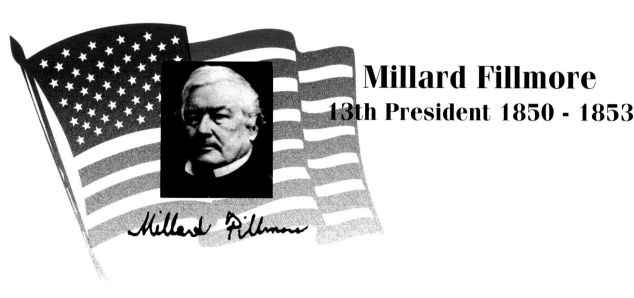

Millard Fillmore
13th President 1850 - 1853

Born: Locke, Cayuga County, New York
January 7, 1800

Died: Buffalo, New York
March 8, 1874

Age at Death: 74

Place of Burial: Forest Lawn Cemetery
Buffalo, New York

NEW YORK

Forest Lawn Cemetery

Born in a log cabin, Millard Fillmore periodically attended public schools until grown. He studied law in Cayuga County and Buffalo, New York, and successfully passed the bar exam. Before practicing law, he taught school and then ran for the New York State Legislature where he served in the Assembly. Subsequently, Fillmore ran for the U. S. House of Representatives and was elected, serving in that capacity until elected Vice President under Zachary Taylor. Fillmore was the last Whig president, failing to receive the nomination of the Whig Party in 1852. Out of office, he later unsuccessfully ran for President on the American Party ticket in 1856, which was known as the "Know Nothing" party because when asked questions about issues, party members would often say they knew nothing about them, in order to avoid controversy.

Fillmore's major accomplishment as president was the sending of Admiral Perry to the far east to open trade with Japan. This act paved the way for expansion of commerce with Asia.

Location:	Forest Lawn Cemetery, 1411 Delaware St. at Delaven St., Buffalo, N.Y.
Burial Facts:	Fillmore is buried in Forest Lawn Cemetery, Buffalo New York with both his first wife, Abigale Powers (died March 30, 1853) and his second wife, Caroline McIntosh, (died August 11, 1881). Fillmore died of debility at age 74.
Graveside Condition:	Forest Lawn is a community cemetery. The grave is well maintained and protected by local agencies.
Directions:	From City Center Buffalo, take Delaware St. (State Highway 384) to Delaven and entrance to Forest Lawn Cemetery. Markers are well-placed indicating gravesite.

Franklin Pierce
14th President 1853 - 1857

Old North County Cemetery

Born:	Hillsboro, New Hampshire November 23, 1804
Died:	Concord, New Hampshire October 8, 1869
Age at Death:	64
Place of Burial:	Old North County Cemetery Concord, New Hampshire

NEW HAMPSHIRE

The only president born, raised, and buried in New Hampshire, Franklin Pierce attended public schools including The Hancock Academy, and Bowdoin College where he received his Bachelor of Arts degree. He studied law in Concord and was admitted to the bar. He served as a member of the bar and later as Speaker of the New Hampshire State legislature, at the same time his father was Governor of New Hampshire. Pierce was subsequently elected to the United States House of Representatives. After a term in the House, he successfully ran for United States Senator. At that time he was the youngest U. S. Senator ever to be elected.

At the outset of the Mexican War, Pierce enlisted as a Private and was quickly promoted to Colonel by President Polk. He served with distinction, rising to the rank of Brigadier General.

A Jacksonian Democrat and States' Rightist, Pierce was a compromise presidential candidate of the Democrats, achieving nomination on the 49th ballot at the nominating convention. When administered the Oath of Office upon his inauguration as president, Pierce was the only president to say," I do solemnly affirm," rather than," I do solemnly swear."

Pierce engineered the Gadsden Purchase which acquired the southern part of Arizona and New Mexico from Mexico. He was not nominated by the Democratic Party after his first term because of his controversial handling of slavery issues.

Location:	North State Street near Capitol Building, Concord, New Hampshire.
Burial Facts:	President Pierce died at the age of 64 as a result of stomach inflammation, and is buried with his wife, Jane Appleton, in the old North County Cemetery, Concord, New Hampshire.
Graveside Condition:	Average care but inadequately protected. Community cemetery, maintained by local operators of cemetery with little embellishment of the President's grave.
Directions:	From Interstate Highway 93, exit Center Street, traveling west to Concord City Center. Pass the State Capitol at North State Street, and travel north on North State Street approximately one quarter mile to Keanes Ave., which is the entrance to the cemetery. The gravesite is in the middle of the cemetery within a wrought-iron fenced area on the north side of the fenced-in area.

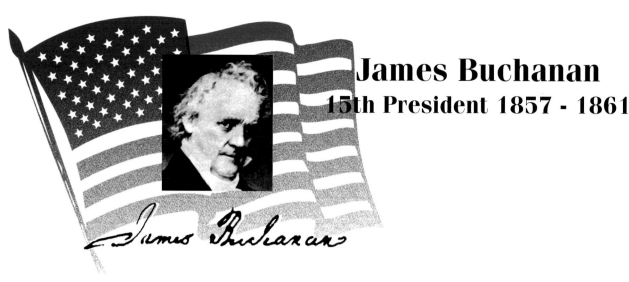

James Buchanan
15th President 1857 - 1861

James Buchanan (signature)

Born: Cove Gap (Mercersburg), Pennsylvania
April 23, 1791

Died: Lancaster, Pennsylvania
June 1, 1868

Age at Death: 77

Place of Burial: Lancaster, Pennsylvania
Woodward Hill Cemetery

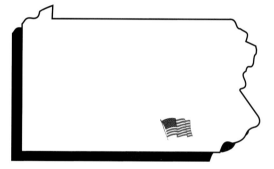

PENNSYLVANIA

Woodward Hill Cemetery

    Another president born on a farm and in a log cabin, Buchanan received his early education at Old Stone Academy in Pennsylvania. During the War of 1812, he enlisted as a private in the Army and served for a short time. Returning to school, he graduated from Dickinson College and then studied law. He was elected to the Pennsylvania Legislature and later served as a congressman in the U. S. House of Representatives. He was Ambassador to Russia, United States Senator, and Secretary of State. He also served as Ambassador to Great Britain.

    Originally a Federalist, Buchanan became a Democrat after the Federalist Party dissolved. He was the only bachelor President and his niece Harriet Lane served as his "first lady."

    Almost immediately after becoming President, Buchanan faced a crisis over slavery which he had the lack of will to confront. He tried to appease the South but alienated the Stephen Douglas branch of the Democratic Party. Buchanan also believed that the federal government was powerless to do anything about slavery. His administrative position therefore weakened his presidency and he lost his party's nomination. Therefore, he did not run for president a second time.

HERE REST THE REMAINS OF
JAMES BUCHANAN
FIFTEENTH PRESIDENT OF THE UNITED STATES.
BORN IN FRANKLIN COUNTY, PA. APRIL 23, 1791.
DIED AT WHEATLAND JUNE 1 1868.

Location: 358 East Strawberry St., Lancaster, Pennsylvania

Burial Facts: James Buchanan died of rheumatic gout at age 77. He is buried in Woodward Hill Cemetery, Lancaster, Pennsylvania, the only president interred in this state.

Graveside Condition: Graveyard is in poor condition with inadequate care and safeguards. There is evidence of vandalism in the cemetery, although the presidential gravesite is in fair condition.

Directions: From "old" downtown Lancaster, Civic Center, travel south on Queen Street from King Street (State Highway 462) approximately three "long" blocks to Chesapeake St. Turn left (east) one-half block to cemetery entrance. *(Note - Even though address is on East Strawberry St., the main entrance gate is sometimes locked. Therefore recommend entering from Chesapeake.) After entering from Chesapeake, drive north up winding road to top of hill. Gravesite will be to the right by a flagpole north of the old carriage house and chapel.

Abraham Lincoln
16th President 1861 - 1865

Abraham Lincoln (signature)

Born: Sinking Spring Farm
Hardin County, Kentucky
February 12, 1809

Died: Washington D. C.
April 15, 1865

Age at Death: 56

Place of Burial: Oak Ridge Cemetery
Springfield, Illinois
May 4, 1865

ILLINOIS

Oak Ridge Cemetery

    Abraham Lincoln was born in a log cabin in Kentucky in 1809. He was tutored and self-educated, being an avid reader and insightful thinker. Lincoln moved to Illinois at a young age and worked as a store clerk, ferry pilot, surveyor and postmaster. For a brief period, Lincoln served as a Captain in the militia during the Black Hawk War. He studied law over the years; passed the bar and went into private practice. He ran for Illinois General Assembly and was elected. He was next elected to the House of Representatives from Illinois and served one term. He sought nomination for Vice President on the Republican Ticket with Fremont in 1855, but failed to receive the nomination. He gained national attention through his debates with Stephen Douglas over the slavery issue while running for United States Senator. Douglas won the U. S. Senate seat over Lincoln but lost to Lincoln in the Presidential election of 1860.

    Lincoln was the first Republican President; the tallest of all presidents at over six feet six inches, and the first president to be assassinated.

Lincoln, unlike Buchanan, believed the national government had the power to deal with the issues of slavery and states' rights. When the Civil War began on April 12, 1861, Lincoln tried in vain to hold the Union together. Slavery, which had been a subordinate issue to preserving the union became of paramount importance as Lincoln came to believe the war could not be successfully concluded without freeing the slaves. He issued the Emancipation Proclamation, and changed the character of the nation forever.

He was plagued with incompetent generals who failed to prosecute the war as it should have been, until he placed Ulysses S. Grant and William T. Sherman in command. After that, the war swung in favor of the north and was brought to a conclusion.

Lincoln was reelected for a second term in 1864 and assassinated at Ford's Theater in Washington D. C. on April 15, 1865.

Location:	Oak Ridge Cemetery, at end of Monument St., off N. Grand Ave.

Location: Oak Ridge Cemetery, at end of Monument St., off N. Grand Ave.

Burial Facts: Lincoln was assassinated at age 56 by John Wilkes Booth at Ford's Theater in Washington D. C. He died in the Petersen Home across the street from Ford's Theater. He was first buried in a crypt located behind the present-day monument where the body remained for approximately six months. The body was then moved to a temporary vault on the hillside nearby the present tomb. During that time, grave robbers tried to remove Lincoln's body to hold it for ransom, but were caught in the act before they had completely removed the coffin. In 1871, Lincoln's remains were transferred to its present location inside the monument at Oak Ridge Cemetery. Lincoln's wife, Mary Todd Lincoln, is also buried in the monument.

Graveside Condition: Excellent. Maintained as a State Historical Site and cared for by Illinois Historic Preservation Agency.

Directions: From Downtown Springfield, travel north on 2nd St. to N. Grand Ave. (approximately 2 miles). Turn left (west) on N. Grand Ave. 1 block to Monument St. Turn right into the cemetery.

Andrew Johnson
17th President 1865 - 1869

Born: Raleigh, North Carolina
December 29, 1808

Died: Carter County, Tennessee
July 31, 1875

Age at Death: 66

Place of Burial: Andrew Johnson National Cemetery
Greeneville, Tennessee

TENNESSEE

Andrew Johnson National Cemetery

The third president to come from Tennessee, Andrew Johnson was the only president to have no formal schooling or tutoring. He was completely self-taught. He apprenticed himself to a tailor at a very early age and went to a neighboring town at age sixteen where he opened his own tailor shop. He ventured into politics first as an alderman, then mayor, and on to the Tennessee State Legislature. He was subsequently elected Governor of Tennessee, to the U. S. House of Representatives, U. S. Senate, and ultimately, Vice President.

Although Andrew Johnson was an opponent of Lincoln's and was a democrat, he was the lone Southern Senator to remain loyal to the union when the south seceded, thereby securing him the nomination for vice president to Lincoln in the election of 1864. When Lincoln was assassinated, Johnson assumed the office of President, but was very ineffective. He began to be at odds with Congress over reconstruction of the south. Because of Johnson's conflicts with Congress, he was the first and only president to be impeached. He was tried by Congress and, even though thirty-six of the fifty-four senators voted to impeach him, the Senate was one vote shy of the two-thirds majority needed to impeach. Johnson remained in office, but did not seek a second term, returning to Tennessee. Six years later he was elected U. S. Senator and returned to Washington. Shortly thereafter he died.

His major achievement as president was the purchase of Alaska from Russia. Johnson was the first president to grant a formal interview with a reporter.

Location:	South of Greeneville in Andrew Johnson National Cemetery on Monument Avenue, Greeneville, Tennessee.
Burial Facts:	Andrew Johnson died of a stroke at age 66. He is buried with his wife, Eliza McCardle in Andrew Johnson National Cemetery, Greeneville, Tennessee.
Graveside Condition:	Excellent. Gravesite sits atop hill in middle of National Cemetery in well-protected monument.
Directions:	Approximately 14 miles southeast of Interstate 81 is Greeneville, Tennessee near the North Carolina border. From Summer Street in downtown Greeneville, travel southwest on Main St. (Tennessee State Highway 93). Go west on U. S. 321 to Monument Avenue. Turn south on Monument, continue one block to cemetery.

Ulysses S. Grant
18th President 1869 - 1877

Born: Point Pleasant, Ohio
April 27, 1822

Died: Mount McGregor, New York
July 23, 1885

Age at Death: 63

Place of Burial: Grant's Tomb
New York City, New York

NEW YORK

Grant's Tomb, Riverside Park, New York, New York

The son of a farmer, Ulysses S. Grant was born in Point Pleasant, Ohio. He attended local schools and then sought congressional appointment to the United States Military Academy at West Point. Grant's real name was Hiram Ulysses Grant, but the congressman who appointed him to West Point thought his first name was Ulysses, and his middle name Simpson (his mother's maiden name). Therefore, he was registered at the military academy as U. S. Grant, and from then on the name stuck. After graduation and commissioning as a Second Lieutenant, he served with General Zachary Taylor in the Mexican War. He married Julia Dent after the Mexican War and was posted to duty in the west but could not take his wife with him. He began to drink and his commanding officer told him he must stop drinking or resign. He resigned.

He returned to civilian life and tried farming, selling real estate, clerking in a leather store, and serving as a custom house clerk. However, he either failed, quit, or was fired from each of these jobs.

When the Civil War broke out he was appointed Colonel in the Army and rose quickly to Brigadier General. In March 1864, Lincoln gave him command of all Northern Armies and he became the best military leader of the North. As a brilliant military commander, Grant and his Generals, Sherman and Sheridan, carried the war to the South and forced Lee's surrender. After the war, Grant returned to Illinois. In 1868 he was drafted by the Republican Party and elected President.

While he was not a particularly effective president, he was honest. However, his political appointees and some in key government positions were disreputable and created chaos through their capricious and sometimes illegal acts.

During Grant's presidency several significant events occurred. President Grant was the first president to talk on the telephone which was invented by Bell in 1876. The first U. S. transcontinental railroad was completed, the Custer massacre occurred at the Little Big Horn, and Congress granted amnesty to most Confederates.

Location:	General Grant National Memorial Riverside Drive and 122nd St. in Manhattan. New York City, New York.
Burial Facts:	President Grant died penniless at the age of 63 due to cancer, and is buried with his wife, Julia Dent, in Grant's Tomb.
Graveside Condition:	Poor condition. There is extensive graffiti on the outside of monument, which is continually removed by park service personnel. The interior of the tomb is well-protected and maintained by Park Service.
Directions:	Arriving in Manhattan via Interstate 80 from New Jersey or Interstate 95 from the east, take Riverside Drive south approximately 37 blocks to 122nd St. The monument sits alone.

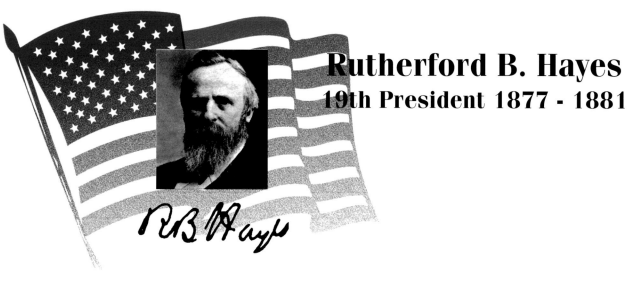

Rutherford B. Hayes
19th President 1877 - 1881

Born: Delaware, Ohio
October 4, 1822

Died: Fremont, Ohio
January 17, 1893

Age at Death: 70

Place of Burial: Spiegel Grove State Park
Fremont, Ohio

OHIO

Rutherford B. Hayes Home
Spiegel Grove State Park
Fremont, Ohio

Rutherford Birchard Hayes was born in 1822 in Delaware, Ohio, where his father farmed. He received formal education at the Academy at Norwalk, and the Isaac Webb School before attending Kenyon College. He graduated from Harvard Law School and returned to Ohio where he practiced law. He entered politics and served as the City Solicitor for the city of Cincinnati and then was elected to the U. S. House of Representatives. He was later elected Governor of Ohio where he helped institute Ohio State University while in office. When the Civil War erupted, Hayes enlisted as a Captain of Volunteers and rose to the rank of Major General. He served in combat and was wounded four times.

In 1876 he ran for President on the Republican ticket. His opponent, Samuel Tildon (Democrat) garnered 4,284,000 votes to Hayes' 4,036,572; however, in the electoral college Hayes won 185 - 184 votes. The election was contested and votes from South Carolina, Florida and Louisiana were challenged. A congressional committee voted 8 to 7 to give Hayes the disputed votes, and he won. Hayes pursued a conciliatory program toward the South and spent a great deal of effort in healing the wounds of the Civil War.

He was the first President to visit the West Coast while in office, traveling 3,000 miles by rail to do so. He also initiated the Easter Egg "roll" on the White House lawn; a tradition still in effect today.

Hayes refused to serve a second term and returned to his home in Ohio where he spent his remaining years involved with humanitarian endeavors.

Location:	1337 Hayes Ave. at Buckland Ave. Fremont, Ohio.
Burial Facts:	Rutherford B. Hayes died of a heart attack at age 70 and is buried with his wife Lucy Webb on the grounds of his home, "Spiegel Grove," Fremont, Ohio.
Graveside Condition:	Well-maintained and protected by State of Ohio Park Service.
Directions:	From State Highway 53 at junction of U. S. Highway 6, travel east on U. S. Highway 6 three miles to Hayes Ave. at Buckland Ave. Approaching from the east, take U. S. Highway 6 to Fremont and proceed through town to Buckland and Hayes.

James A. Garfield
20th President
March 4, 1881 - Sept. 19, 1881

Born: Orange Township
Moreland (Moreland Hills), Ohio
November 19, 1831

Died: Elberton, New Jersey
September 19, 1881

Age at Death: 49

Place of Burial: Lake View Cemetery
Cleveland, Ohio

OHIO

Garfield Monument
Lake View Cemetery

The last President born in a log cabin, James Abram Garfield was born on his father's farm in northeastern Ohio. Even as a lad, Garfield valued education and he attended school eagerly. He attended Geauga Academy, Western Reserve Eclectic Institute and graduated from Williams College in 1856. He then became a school teacher and later President of Hiram College, until the advent of the Civil War, when he was commissioned Lt. Colonel of the 42nd Ohio Volunteers. He served with distinction and rose to the rank of Major General, being the youngest Major General to serve in the Northern Army in the Civil War. While in the army, he was elected to the House of Representatives by the voters back in Ohio. He rose to House Minority Leader and was nominated by the Republican Party in 1880 as a compromise candidate. He won an easy victory over his Democratic opponent, William S. Hancock.

The only president who was an ordained minister (Disciple of Christ Church), he could write Latin with one hand and Greek with the other at the same time. He was the first left-handed president and the first to have his mother live in the White House.

On July 2, 1881, Garfield was shot by Charles J. Guiteau, a disappointed office seeker, in the Baltimore and Potomac train depot in Washington D. C. He lingered for two months, during which time he was moved to Elberton, New Jersey, where he died of gunshot wound complications and septicemia (blood poisoning).

Location:　　Lake View Cemetery, 12316 Euclid Ave. at 123rd St. Cleveland, Ohio.

Burial Facts:　　James Abram Garfield died as a result of complications from an assassin's bullet at age 49. He is buried with his wife Lucretia Rudolph Garfield in the basement of the monument. Garfield's casket is the only one on display and permanently draped with an American flag.

Graveside Condition:　　Excellent. Built of native Ohio sandstone. Located in public cemetery. Maintained by Lake View Cemetery Association. Informative docent tours are regularly presented.

Directions:　　From downtown Cleveland take Euclid Ave. (Highway 20) east to E. 123rd St. Lake View Cemetery Entrance

Chester A. Arthur
21st President 1881 - 1885

Born: Fairfield, Vermont
October 5, 1830

Died: New York, New York
November 18, 1886

Age at Death: 56

Place of Burial: Rural Cemetery
Albany, New York

NEW YORK

Rural Cemetery, Albany, New York

The son of northern Irish immigrants, Chester Alan Arthur was born in Vermont. He attended public schools and the Lyceum School before matriculating to Union College where he graduated with honors. He was a Phi Beta Kappa scholar as were John Quincy Adams, Theodore Roosevelt, and George Bush; however he was the only one to graduate from a non-Ivy League School.

After leaving Union College, Arthur taught school and served as a school principal while he studied law, subsequently passing the bar and becoming a practicing attorney.

During the Civil War, he was commissioned as Quartermaster General for New York, providing much needed supplies for Union troops. After the war he was appointed to the post of New York Collector of Customs and was picked by the Republican party as President Garfield's running mate. After Garfield's assassination, Arthur became President and reformed the old patronage system by passage of the Civil Service law. He is also credited with modernizing the U. S. Navy and U. S. Postal System.

Denied renomination by his party, because of political reforms, Arthur left office at the end of his term and returned to Albany where he died one year later.

Location:	Cemetery Ave., off Broadway. Menands (a suburb of Albany), New York.
Burial Facts:	Chester Alan Arthur died of cerebral hemorrhage and Bright's Disease at age 56. He is buried with his wife, Ellen L. Herndon Arthur, in the Albany Rural Cemetery, Albany, New York. Arthur's angel guarded sarcophagus is the most unusual of all the President's final resting place.
Graveside Condition:	Fair. Burial site is maintained and protected by community cemetery personnel.
Directions:	From downtown Albany, take State Route 32 northeast approximately two and one half miles to Menands (a suburb of Albany). Travel north on Broadway to Chatham St. Turn west approximately one mile to cemetery . Take second entrance to gravesite. Stop at Caretaker's office just inside entrance for map to the gravesite.

Grover Cleveland
22nd and 24th President
1885 - 1889 & 1893-1897

Born: Caldwell, New Jersey
March 18, 1837

Died: Princeton, New Jersey
June 24, 1908

Age at Death: 71

Place of Burial: Princeton Cemetery
Princeton, New Jersey

NEW JERSEY

Princeton Cemetery, Princeton, New Jersey

Son of a Presbyterian minister, Grover Cleveland, (whose full name was Stephen Grover Cleveland), was the only President to serve two nonconsecutive terms. After attending public schools, Cleveland studied law in Buffalo, New York, and began law practice. Cleveland served in several public offices including Sheriff of Erie County, New York and Assistant District Attorney for Erie County, New York. He was elected mayor of Buffalo and in 1882, Governor of New York.

The Democratic Party nominated him for both of his terms of office and he defeated James G. Blaine in 1884. Cleveland was then defeated by Benjamin Harrison in 1888, who he in turn defeated in the election of 1892.

Considered an honest and incorruptible man, Cleveland pushed Civil Service reform; opposed pension fraud and high tariffs. While President, he had a secret operation for mouth cancer on a yacht off the coast of Long Island, a little known fact unique in Presidential annals. Grover Cleveland was the only president to have a child actually born inside the White House. After his second term, he retired to Princeton University where he turned to lecturing at the University and serving as a trustee.

Location:	Princeton Cemetery, Princeton, New Jersey, Witherspoon and Wiggins Streets.
Burial Facts:	Grover Cleveland is buried in the Princeton Cemetery, Princeton, New Jersey. He died of a heart attack at age 71. His wife Frances Folsom Cleveland is also buried in the Princeton Cemetery, next to her husband.
Graveside Condition:	Good. Gravesite is maintained and protected by cemetery personnel in the community cemetery.
Directions:	From downtown Princeton at the University, take Witherspoon St. east to Wiggins and the cemetery.

Benjamin Harrison
23rd President 1889 - 1893

Born: North Bend, Ohio
August 20, 1833

Died: Indianapolis, Indiana
March 13, 1901

Age at Death: 67

Place of Burial: Crown Hill Cemetery
Indianapolis, Indiana

INDIANA

Crown Hill Cemetery

Benjamin Harrison was named for his great-grandfather, a signer of the Declaration of Independence. His grandfather, William Henry Harrison, was ninth U. S. President, making William Henry Harrison and Benjamin Harrison the only grandfather-grandson presidents.

Benjamin Harrison grew up on his father's farm, receiving private tutoring until he attended Farmers College. He later earned his Bachelor of Arts degree from Miami (Ohio) University and then proceeded to study law. He was a practicing attorney in Indiana and served as a notary public.

During the Civil War, Benjamin Harrison was appointed the rank of Colonel in the 70th Indiana Volunteers, rising to the rank of Brigadier General. After the war he returned to his law practice in Indiana.

He received the Republican nomination on the eighth ballot and went on to defeat Cleveland in the general election of 1888. Although he was behind in the popular vote, he won the electoral college vote by 65 votes.

As president, Harrison failed to please either reformers or party bosses and began to lose party support. His first wife, Caroline Scott Harrison, died in the White House in 1892. He married her niece, Mary Scott Dimmick in 1896. After the presidency, Benjamin Harrison returned to his law practice in Indianapolis.

Location:	Crown Hill Cemetery, 700 W. 38th St., Indianapolis, Indiana.
Burial Facts:	Benjamin Harrison died of pneumonia at age 67 and is buried in Crown Hill Cemetery, Indianapolis, along with his first and second wives.
Graveside Condition:	Good condition. Well-preserved and maintained by community cemetery personnel.
Directions:	Taking Interstate 65 northwest from downtown Indianapolis, take exit #7 for Northwestern Ave. Travel approximately 6 blocks northwest to West 38th St. Turn east approximately 2 blocks to cemetery entrance. Enter southern entrance and follow signs to section 13.

William McKinley
25th President 1897 - 1901

Born: Niles, Ohio
January 29, 1843

Died: Buffalo, New York
September 14, 1901

Age at Death: 58

Place of Burial: Canton, Ohio

OHIO

William McKinley Monument
Westland Cemetery

The last Civil War veteran to serve as president, William McKinley enlisted as a Private in the Ohio 23rd Volunteers in 1861, and rose to the rank of Major. Both Rutherford B. Hayes and McKinley served in the same regiment during the Civil War and saw combat.

McKinley attended public schools early in life and was then enrolled in the Poland Seminary where he attended until transferring to Allegheny College in Pennsylvania. He left Allegheny College and became a teacher in a country school.

After his service in the Civil War, he returned to Canton, Ohio, studied law, and was admitted to the bar as an attorney. He ran for Congress and was elected to the U. S. House of Representatives where he served six terms. In 1892 he was elected Governor of Ohio, serving in that capacity until his nomination for President in 1896.

McKinley ran his campaign from his front porch because his wife was an invalid and he refused to leave her to travel the country campaigning. During his Presidency, Cuba was still a colony of Spain. Many newspaper editors and other people wanted McKinley to declare war on Spain and free Cuba. War was declared April 11, 1898 and 100 days later Spain was defeated in Cuba as well as in the Philippines, Guam, & Puerto Rico. Also during his term Hawaii was annexed and became an American Territory.

After reelection in 1900, McKinley attended the Pan American Exposition in Buffalo in September where he was assassinated at a reception by Leon Czolgosz, an anarchist, who was tried and later executed.

Location:	McKinley State Memorial Park and Tomb, Westland Cemetery, 7th St. N. W. Canton, Ohio
Burial Facts:	President McKinley was shot by an assassin on September 6, 1901. He died at age 58 as a result of his wounds on Sept. 14, 1901, only six months into his second term of office. He is buried with his wife Ida Saxton McKinley at Canton Ohio.
Graveside Condition:	Excellent. Maintained and protected by State of Ohio Parks Service.
Directions:	Take Exit 106 off Interstate 77. Turn east on 12th St. The cemetery is next to the freeway. Follow memorial signs to 7th St. N. W.

Theodore Roosevelt
26th President 1901-1909

Born: New York City, New York
October 27, 1858

Died: Oyster Bay, New York
January 6, 1919

Age at Death: 60

Place of Burial: Young's Memorial Cemetery
Oyster Bay, N.Y.

NEW YORK

Young's Memorial Cemetery, Oyster Bay, N.Y.

Theodore Roosevelt was the fifth Vice President to succeed to the presidency due to the death of his predecessor, William McKinley. Roosevelt had served as New York State Assemblyman, U.S. Civil Service Commissioner, President of the New York Board of Police Commissioners, Assistant Secretary of the Navy, Governor of New York, and Vice President of the United States of America.

During the Spanish American War in 1898, he organized a volunteer regiment of cowboys and cavalry men known as the Rough Riders, and fought in Cuba against the Spanish. Roosevelt attained the rank of Colonel of the First U.S. Volunteer Cavalry Regiment during the Spanish American War.

Theodore, nicknamed "Teddy," had the teddy bear named after him, was the first president to fly in an airplane, and was the youngest man to serve as president, being elevated to that position at the age of 42 by McKinley's assassination. He was the first American to win a Nobel Prize, winning the Nobel Peace Prize in 1906 for bringing the Russo-Japanese war to an end.

Location:	3 miles northeast of Oyster Bay on Long Island, New York, on Cove Neck Road.
Burial facts:	President Theodore Roosevelt died of a coronary embolism on January 6, 1919. He left his second wife, Edith, and four children: Theodore (1887-1944), Kermit (1889-1943), Ethel Carow (1891-1977), Archibald (1894-1979). A son, Quentin (1897-1918) was killed in World War I. President Roosevelt is buried in Young's Memorial Cemetery on a forested hillside in Oyster Bay, New York, near his "Sagamore Hill" homesite, where he had lived for 40 years.
Gravesite Condition:	Excellent. Well maintained by Estate Staff. Surrounding graves also well-maintained. No vandalism noted.
Directions:	Approaching from the north on Interstate 95, take Interstate 295 to Long Island, and join East Interstate 495. Approaching from the west (Manhattan) take Interstate 495 to Long Island. Travel east on Interstate 495 to Glen Cove Exit, travel north on Glen Cove approximately 1.7 miles to North Hemstead Rd. (also known as State Highway 25A) and travel approximately 7 miles to Cove Road. Turn north on Cove Road and travel approximately 2 miles to Theodore Roosevelt Gravesite in Young's Memorial Cemetery. A small parking lot is located on the west side of Cove Road at the front of the cemetery.

Errata: Pres. Theodore Roosevelt, page 60.

Alice Longworth, eldest of Theodore Roosevelt's five (not four) children, outlived all of her siblings.

Directions: P. James Roosevelt, President, Youngs Memorial Cemetery Corporation, corresponded that an easier route is: Take 495, L.I. Expressway to exit 41, 106 and 107 Northbound. Stay to the right on 106 when they divide. Follow 106 North (across 25A and about 7 miles into Oyster Bay). Turn right (east) in Oyster Bay at traffic light at intersection of East Main St. - marked also by a sign to Sagamore Hill. (East Main Street changes its name to Oyster Bay Cove Rd. Stay on it.) Proceed 1 1/2 miles from traffic light to small Cemetery parking lot on the right, opposite the intersection of Cove Neck Road.

William Howard Taft
27th President 1909 - 1913

Born: Cincinnati, Ohio
September 15, 1857

Died: Washington, D. C.
March 8, 1930

Age at Death: 72

Place of Burial: Arlington National Cemetery
Arlington, Virginia

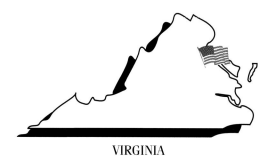

VIRGINIA

Arlington National Cemetery

The largest President at over six feet in height and 300 pounds, William Howard Taft was the first president to have an official automobile, the first to play golf, and establish the tradition of the President's throwing out the first ball at the beginning of baseball season. He was the only President to keep cows on the White House lawn.

Taft attended Woodward Hill School as a lad and at age 17 entered Yale University where he earned his Bachelor's degree. He later attended Cincinnati Law School, earning his law degree in 1880, and opening his law practice thereafter. He became a prosecuting attorney for Hamilton County, Ohio, then an Ohio Superior Court Judge. He was later a U. S. Solicitor General, then elevated to Judge of the Federal Circuit Court. After the Spanish-American War, he was appointed Civil Governor of the Philippines and subsequently Secretary of War under Theodore Roosevelt.

Taft was an able and competent judge as well as an effective Governor while serving in the Philippines. He was Theodore Roosevelt's handpicked successor in 1908 and won handily over William Jennings Bryan. Although he carried on Theodore Roosevelt's programs he lost favor with the progressive wing of the Republican Party and was defeated by both Theodore Roosevelt, running on the Bull Moose ticket, and Woodrow Wilson, the Democratic Candidate in the election of 1912.

After leaving office in 1913, Taft was appointed Chief Justice of the U. S. Supreme Court by President Harding and served as such until his retirement in 1930 just prior to his death. He is the only president to have held the office of Supreme Court Justice.

Location: Through Entrance Gate from Memorial Drive off Jefferson Davis Highway, Arlington National Cemetery, VA

Burial Facts: William Howard Taft died of debility at age 72 in 1930. He is buried in Arlington National Cemetery with his wife Hellen Herron.

Graveside Condition: Excellent. Maintained and protected by National Cemetery personnel.

Directions: From Washington D. C., travel southwest over Arlington Memorial Bridge to Jefferson Davis Highway straight into Entrance Gate of Arlington Cemetery. From Virginia, travel east on U. S. Highway 50 to Jefferson Davis Highway. Travel southeast approximately one-third mile to cemetery Entrance Gate on west side of freeway.

Woodrow Wilson
28th President 1913 - 1921

Born: Staunton, Virginia
December 28, 1856

Died: Washington D. C.
February 3, 1924

Age at Death: 67

Place of Burial: National Cathedral
Washington, D. C.

WASHINGTON, D.C.

The National Cathedral

Thomas Woodrow Wilson is the only president buried in Washington D. C. He was also the only president to reside in Washington D. C. after leaving office. He was the last president to travel to his inauguration in a horse and carriage and to use this mode of conveyance. During his tenure in office, the official Presidential Flag was adopted, and he was the first president to speak on radio.

Woodrow Wilson was born in the parsonage of his father's church in Staunton, Virginia. His father was a Presbyterian minister, having an early influence on his son's values and ideas. Wilson received private tutoring until entering Davidson College. He attended Princeton University, obtaining his Bachelor of Arts degree. While at Princeton, Wilson played football and later acted as an assistant coach.

After receiving his law degree from University of Virginia Law School, he practiced law in Atlanta, Georgia. He returned to school and earned a Ph.D. in political science from John Hopkins University and began a teaching career. He was the only president to have earned a doctoral degree. In 1902 he became President of Princeton University.

In 1910, Wilson was elected Governor of New Jersey. Two years after election as Governor, he received the Democratic Party nomination, defeating William Howard Taft (Republican) and Theodore Roosevelt (Progressive Party) in the Presidential election of 1912.

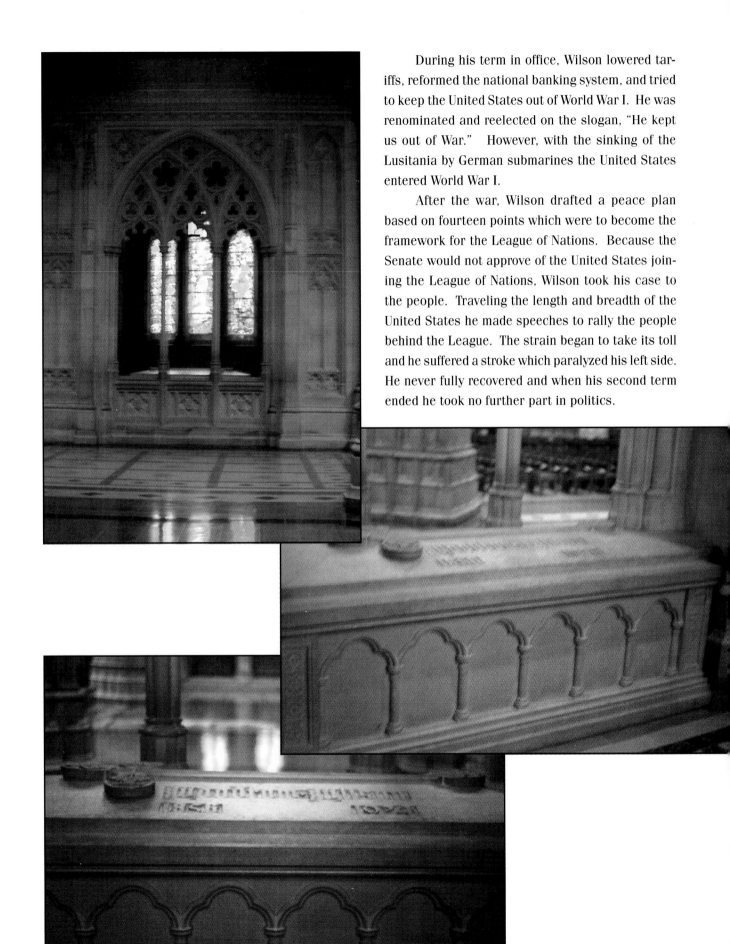

During his term in office, Wilson lowered tariffs, reformed the national banking system, and tried to keep the United States out of World War I. He was renominated and reelected on the slogan, "He kept us out of War." However, with the sinking of the Lusitania by German submarines the United States entered World War I.

After the war, Wilson drafted a peace plan based on fourteen points which were to become the framework for the League of Nations. Because the Senate would not approve of the United States joining the League of Nations, Wilson took his case to the people. Traveling the length and breadth of the United States he made speeches to rally the people behind the League. The strain began to take its toll and he suffered a stroke which paralyzed his left side. He never fully recovered and when his second term ended he took no further part in politics.

Location:	Southside of Nave of Washington National Cathedral, Wisconsin and Massachusetts Ave. N.W., Washington D. C.
Burial Facts:	Having died of apoplexy at age 67, Woodrow Wilson was interred in the Nave of the National Cathedral in Washington D. C. His first wife, Ellen Axson Wilson is buried in Rome, Georgia. His second wife, Edith Galt Wilson, is buried in the National Cathedral one crypt below him.
Graveside Condition:	Excellent. Maintained and protected by Cathedral staff.
Directions:	From downtown Washington D. C. travel northwest on Massachusetts Avenue to Wisconsin Avenue. Turn north on Wisconsin one block to parking lot entrance.

Warren G. Harding
29th President 1921 - 1923

Born: Blooming Grove (Corsica), Ohio
           November 2, 1865

Died: San Francisco, California
         August 2,1923

Age at Death: 57

Place of Burial: Harding Memorial
           Marion, Ohio

OHIO

Warren G. Harding Memorial

     William Gamaliel Harding was a typical small-town Ohio youth of that day. He quit school at age 17, taught in a rural school, worked at a weekly paper in Marion, Ohio, and then bought a newspaper called the "Star." He had attended Ohio Central College and married Florence De Wolfe in 1891. His early political offices included memberships in the Ohio State Senate and the Lt. Governorship of Ohio. After serving in the U. S. Senate for six years he was nominated by the Republican Party and elected President. His cabinet had some able, honest men, but also some manifestly unfit to hold office. The imminent scandal over the Tea Pot Dome oil reserves and the Veterans' Bureau practices resulted in indictments of some of his cabinet members. He died suddenly upon his return from Alaska in 1923. Several significant events occurred during his Presidency. His election was the first to have the results broadcast over radio, and also he was the first to ride in an automobile to a Presidential inauguration. He dedicated the Tomb of the Unknown Soldier at Arlington National Cemetery and women were allowed to vote for the first time in a national election.

Location:	At Delaware Avenue and Vernon Heights Blvd., Marion, Ohio.
Burial Facts:	Dead at age 57 from apoplexy, Harding was buried in the Blooming Grove section of Marion, Ohio. He is buried with his wife, Florence De Wolfe Harding in stone coffins in the inner garden of the memorial.
Graveside Condition:	Well-maintained and protected by Memorial Foundation.
Directions:	From Highway U. S. 23, take State Rt. 95 west approximately two miles to Vernon Heights Blvd. Turn south one-half block at Delaware Ave.

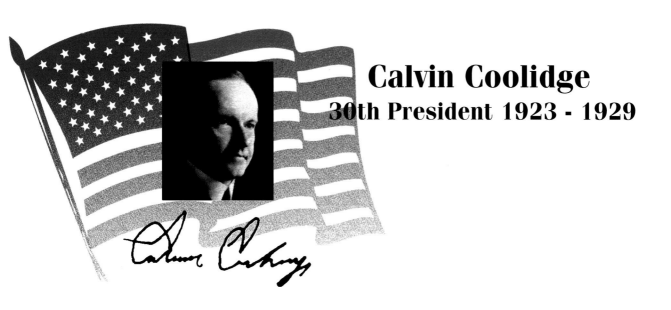

Calvin Coolidge
30th President 1923 - 1929

Born: Plymouth Notch, Vermont
July 4, 1872

Died: Northampton, Massachusetts
January 5, 1933

Age at Death: 60

Place of Burial: Plymouth Notch Cemetery
Plymouth, Vermont

VERMONT

Plymouth Notch Cemetery

Upon the death of President Warren G. Harding, Calvin Coolidge was sworn into office by his father Colonel John Coolidge, a Justice of the Peace, making him the only President administered the oath of office by his father.

Coolidge was born John Calvin Coolidge, the only son of John and Victoria Coolidge. He attended public schools, and graduated from Amherst College. He studied law in Northampton, Massachusetts, passing the bar in 1897. He became interested in politics at a young age and served as a member of the Massachusetts State House of Representatives. Later, he was elected Mayor of Northampton, served in the State Senate, was Lt. Governor, then Governor before being elected to U. S. Vice President on the same ticket as Harding. When Harding died, Coolidge calmly and without fanfare assumed the Office of President, while continuing Harding's programs.

In 1924 Coolidge ran for election in his own right and was elected by a sizeable majority. The economy was booming and wages were high. He was highly regarded by most Americans, but when the election of 1928 neared he said, "I do not choose to run."

During Coolidge's term in office, Lindbergh flew alone across the Atlantic. President Coolidge was the first President seen in newsreels in the theaters, and gave the first inaugural address heard over the radio.

Location:	One mile southwest of Plymouth, Vermont, on south side of Vermont Route 100A.
Burial Facts:	Coolidge died at age 60 of coronary thrombosis. He is buried in the public cemetery at Plymouth, Vermont, in the Plymouth Notch Cemetery along with his wife, Grace Goodhue Coolidge, who died in 1957.
Graveside Condition:	Condition good. Maintained and protected by local community cemetery personnel.
Directions:	Plymouth, Vermont, is approximately 20 miles west-south-west of the junction of Interstate 89 and 91 on the Vermont New Hampshire border, via U. S. Highway 4 to State Highway 100 A. Take State Rt. 100A southwest to Plymouth, and continue approximately one mile to Plymouth Notch Cemetery Road.

Herbert Hoover
31st President 1929 - 1933

Born: West Branch, Iowa
            August 10, 1874

Died: New York City, New York
            October 20, 1964

Age at Death: 90

Place of Burial: West Branch, Iowa

IOWA

President Hoover Memorial Burial Site

The first President born west of the Mississippi River, Herbert Clark Hoover was the first President (along with Eisenhower) who was not of English, Irish, or Dutch ancestry. Hoover and Eisenhower were both German descendents. Hoover's father and mother both died by the time he was eight years old and he was raised by an uncle in Oregon. He attended local schools and later, Stanford University in California. After graduating from Stanford with a degree in engineering, Hoover went to Australia and developed a gold mine which brought him a good deal of wealth.

During World War I when many people in German-occupied Belgium were starving, Hoover helped bring food from the U. S. saving millions from starvation. When the U. S. entered World War I President Wilson appointed Hoover Food Administrator because of his ability to get people to save food for the war effort.

President Harding appointed him Secretary of Commerce. Hoover had never run for any political office but was elected President in 1928 by a large majority based on his previous humanitarian work.

He was the first President to authorize construction of an aircraft carrier even though he was a Quaker. Then with the crash of the stock market in 1929, the country sank into a great depression with businesses failing and people out of work. The public blamed Hoover even though he was not directly to blame and he lost the election of 1932.

Location:	On the grounds of the Herbert Hoover Presidential Library and Museum, West Branch, Iowa.
Burial Facts:	President Hoover died at age 90 of an internal hemorrhage in New York City in 1964 and is buried on a hill overlooking the Herbert Hoover Presidential Library and Museum along with his wife Lou Henry in West Branch, Iowa.
Graveside Condition:	Excellent: Preserved, protected, and maintained by National Park Service.
Directions:	Located in West Branch, Iowa, the Herbert Hoover National Historic Site is on Parkside Drive and Main St., one-half mile north from Exit 254 off Interstate Highway 80. Roadway to gravesite is located approximately one block south of Visitor Center.

Franklin Delano Roosevelt
32nd President 1933 - 1945

Born: Hyde Park, New York
January 30, 1882

Died: Warm Springs, Georgia
April 12, 1945

Age at Death: 63

Place of Burial: Hyde Park, New York

NEW YORK

Hyde Park

Having been elected President to more terms (four) than any other president, Franklin Delano Roosevelt had the greatest impact on the country since Abraham Lincoln. A Democrat, Roosevelt, affectionately known as F. D. R., was born to a wealthy family on his father's estate in Hyde Park, New York.

He was distantly related to ten other presidents: Washington, John Adams, John Quincy Adams, James Madison, Martin Van Buren, William Henry Harrison, Benjamin Harrison, Zachary Taylor, U. S. Grant, and William Howard Taft. He was a fifth cousin to Theodore Roosevelt and his wife Eleanor Roosevelt was also a distant cousin. British Prime Minister Winston Churchill, and General of the Army Douglas MacArthur, were also distant relatives. (FDR and Churchill had the same maternal-great-grandmother, Nellie Belcher.)

FDR was privately tutored until he attended Groton School. He earned his Bachelor's degree from Harvard University and studied law at Columbia University in New York City. He practiced law until he ran for State Senator, winning a seat in the New York State Senate.

During World War I he was appointed Assistant Secretary of the Navy by President Wilson. After the war he ran on the Democratic ticket with James Cox and was defeated by Republican Harding.

In 1921 he suffered the physically debilitating disease, polio, which left him crippled for the rest of his life and confined to a wheel chair. FDR underwent rehabilitation and when he had regained partial use of his legs, he ran for Governor of New York and was elected.

In 1929 the stock market "crashed" and a great depression struck America. Roosevelt won the Democratic nomination for president and defeated Herbert Hoover in 1932.

The newly elected president immediately initiated the recovery from the depression by aggressive federal programs such as a Civilian Conservation Corps (CCC), Works Progress Administration (WPA), and Social Security. He was President during World War II and rallied the country to totally support the war effort. He was instrumental in creating the United Nations and met with Churchill and Stalin on two occasions to consolidate the Allied effort against the Axis. Thus he became the first President to leave this country during wartime.

Roosevelt had four sons: John, James, Elliot, and Franklin Delano Jr., each of which served as officers in the Army, Marines, or Navy during World War II. Roosevelt was the last President inaugurated in March, as a constitutional amendment was passed in 1933 moving the inaugural date back to January. Roosevelt died on April 12, 1945, less than a month before the end of World War II in Europe and less than five months before the end of the war against Japan.

Location:	511 Albany Post Road, one mile south of Hyde Park, New York on U. S. Highway 9.
Burial Facts:	Franklin Roosevelt died at age 63 of a cerebral hemorrhage in Warm Springs, Georgia. He is buried with his wife Eleanor Roosevelt in the Rose Garden at Hyde Park, New York.
Graveside Condition:	Excellent. Maintained and protected by National Archives and Records Administration.
Directions:	From Hyde Park on the east bank of the Hudson River, leave south on U. S. Highway 9 to Franklin D. Roosevelt Home, Library and Museum . Gravesite is in Rose Garden on Hyde Park Estate grounds. Guided tours to Hyde Park home are available. Shaded picnic tables located near parking lot.

Harry S. Truman
33rd President 1945 - 1953

Courtyard, Truman Library
Independence, Missouri

Born: Lamar, Missouri
May 8, 1884

Died: Kansas City Missouri
December 26, 1972

Age at Death: 86

Place of Burial: Independence, Missouri

MISSOURI

Harry S. Truman, (the initial "S" did not stand for any name), was born in Lamar, Missouri on his father's farm. Harry had to wear glasses from age eight and as a result could not participate in rugged games like other boys. Instead, he read everything he could. After graduating from high school, he worked on the railroad, at a bank, and on the family farm. He was the only president in the twentieth century who did not attend college.

When the United States entered World War I Truman, who was an artillery Captain in the Missouri National Guard, volunteered to go to France. He was one of only two presidents to serve in the military in World War I. He served with honor, returning to Kansas City, Missouri after the war. He married Bess (Elizabeth Wallace) and opened a clothing store in Kansas City. When the business failed, he entered politics and was elected County Judge. In 1934 he was elected to the U. S. Senate and subsequently was chosen by FDR for vice president in 1944. When FDR died suddenly, Truman was faced with finishing World War II. He ordered the first atomic bombs to be dropped on Hiroshima and Nagasaki Japan in order to hasten the end of the war and save lives which would most likely have been lost in an invasion of Japan. He helped solidify the United Nations and opened the first U. N. meeting in San Francisco. In 1950 the North Koreans invaded South Korea and Truman ordered U. S. troops to help save South Korea from Communism under the auspices of the United Nations.

Truman did not run for reelection in 1952, instead he retired to Independence, Missouri to write his memoirs.

Highlights of his administration included the initiation of the "Marshall" plan, which aided in the recovery of Europe after the second World War. In 1948 he scored the greatest upset in presidential election history. The polls all showed Thomas Dewey would win, but Truman won the election, in spite of the predictions.

Location: Delaware St. and U. S. Highway 24, Independence, Missouri.

Burial Facts: Harry Truman died of debility at age 86 in 1972. He is buried at the Harry S. Truman Library and Museum in Independence, MO next to his wife Bess Wallace Truman.

Graveside Condition: Excellent. Preserved and maintained by National Archives and Records

Directions: 12 miles east of Kansas City in Independence, Missouri. Take U. S. Highway 24 to Delaware St. Turn north to Museum, Library, and gravesite, which is located in the courtyard of the complex.

Dwight David Eisenhower
34th President 1953 - 1961

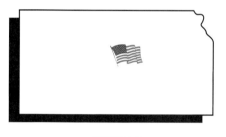

Born: Denison, Texas
October 14, 1890

Died: Walter Reed Hospital, Washington D. C.
March 28, 1969

Age at Death: 78

Place of Burial: Abilene, Kansas

KANSAS

Eisenhower Library and Museum Complex

Dwight David Eisenhower was originally named David Dwight but through common usage and choice, the names were switched. However, his nickname "Ike" was that by which the world honored him.

Soon after Dwight David Eisenhower was born, his family moved from Texas to Kansas. He attended local schools and when he took the exam for the Navy Academy, he marked either West Point or Annapolis as his choice for attending, ending up at the U. S. Military Academy (West Point). Ike played football at West Point until he injured his knee. Upon graduating during World War I he served as training officer in the United States. Later he served on the staffs of General John Pershing and Douglas MacArthur. It was during this period that Eisenhower learned to fly, making him the first President to become a licensed pilot. After World War II broke out, President Roosevelt promoted him over 366 other officers and gave him command of U. S. Forces fighting in North Africa. Subsequently he was named Supreme Allied Commander of all Allied Forces in Europe. He organized the D-Day landings in France, the largest amphibian landing in world history. After WWII he served as President of Columbia University but returned to the service to become NATO Commander. Shortly after his 1952 election to President he flew to Korea, and through his efforts, achieved an end to the hostilities.

As President he continued many of the policies of Roosevelt and Truman. He fully integrated the Armed Forces and when the Governor of Arkansas failed to obey integration laws at Little Rock High School, he sent in Federal Troops and accomplished the integration. During his administration the space race began. Russia launched the first satellite, Sputnik, soon followed by the United States Explorer I satellite. During his time in office, Alaska and Hawaii were the last two states to be included in the Union. He held the first televised news conference and was seen continually on television, whether speaking to the nation or on the golf course playing his favorite sport. Upon retirement day of 1961, he retired to live on his farm in Gettysburg, Pennsylvania, the first home he ever owned.

Location: 201 SE. 4th Street, Abilene, Kansas.

Burial Facts: Succumbing to a heart attack at age 78, Eisenhower was buried at his boyhood home of Abilene, Kansas. He and his wife Mamie Dodd Eisenhower are entombed together in the chapel on the grounds of the museum and library.

Graveside Condition: Excellent. Maintained and protected by National Archives and Records Administration.

Directions: From Interstate 70, Abilene Kansas, travel South 2 miles on State Rt. 15, (Buckeye St.) to 4th St. Turn east 1 block to grounds.

John Fitzgerald Kennedy
35th President 1961 - Nov. 22, 1963

Born: Brookline, Massachusetts
May 29, 1917

Died: Dallas, Texas
November 22, 1963

Age at Death: 46

Place of Burial: Arlington National Cemetery
Arlington, Virginia

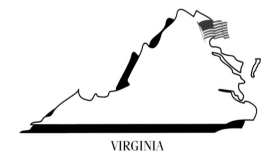

VIRGINIA

Arlington National Cemetery

The first President born in the 20th century, John Kennedy was one of nine children born to Joseph and Rose Kennedy. His father was Ambassador to England under President Franklin Roosevelt. Kennedy graduated from Harvard, and completed further studies at Princeton and Stanford. When World War II began he joined the navy and saw action in the South Pacific area as a PT Boat Commander. He was rammed by a Japanese Destroyer and spent several days marooned on a desert island. He was the only president to receive wounds in action in World War II. He was decorated for saving a member of his crew by towing him to shore. After the war, while recuperating in a hospital from surgery on his back which was injured in World War II, he wrote the prize-winning book, Profiles in Courage.

He successfully ran for both the House of Representatives from Massachusetts and subsequently, the U. S. Senate. Gaining national prominence, he ran for president in 1960, defeating Vice President Nixon by a slim majority in the closest Presidential race in history. In the course of the campaign, the first televised presidential debates occurred.

At age 43 he was the youngest to be elected president, and he was the first Roman Catholic to be elected to the Presidency.

Highlights of his administration included the establishment of the Peace Corps, the unsuccessful invasion of Cuba in April, 1961, the Cuban Missile Crisis of 1962, when he blockaded Cuba and forced Russia to back down and withhold their missiles.

While riding through Dallas in an open sedan, en route to make a speech, he was shot by Lee Harvey Oswald. He was the fourth President to be assassinated in office.

Location: South Gate, Arlington National Cemetery, Arlington, Virginia.

Burial Facts: John Kennedy is buried in Arlington National Cemetery as a result of gunshot wounds received when assassinated by Lee Harvey Oswald in 1963. His brother Robert Kennedy, (JFK's Attorney General, and 1968 candidate for President) is buried nearby, also a victim of an assassin's bullet. His wife, Jacqueline Bouvier Kennedy Onassis, who died May 19, 1994, is buried with him.

Graveside Condition: Excellent. Maintained and protected by Park Service Personnel. Note: An eternal flame burns continuously at the gravesite.

Directions: From Washington D. C., travel southwest over Arlington Memorial Bridge to Jefferson Davis Highway straight into Entrance Gate of Arlington Cemetery. From Virginia, travel east on U. S. Highway 50 to Jefferson Davis Highway. Travel southeast approximately one-third mile to cemetery Entrance Gate on west side of freeway.

Lyndon Baines Johnson
36th President 1963 - 1969

Born: Stonewall, Texas
August 27, 1908

Died: Stonewall, Texas
January 22, 1973

Age at Death: 64

Place of Burial: Stonewall, Texas

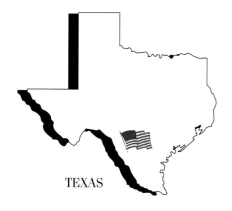

TEXAS

Family Cemetery

Born of parents who were both school teachers and whose father and grandfather had been members of the Texas legislature, Lyndon Johnson attended San Marcos College and taught school upon graduation. At age 29, he ran for Congress and was elected to the House of Representatives. Shortly after the Japanese bombed Pearl Harbor, Johnson, a reserve Naval Officer, requested active duty with the Navy. He was the first member of Congress to go into uniform. After World War II, he was elected to the U. S. Senate. He was a great U. S. Senator who could get things done and get people with opposing ideas to work together.

He was elected Vice President in 1960 and became president when JFK was assassinated in Dallas. He was the first Vice President to be present when a President was killed. He was also the first to be sworn in on an airplane, and the first sworn in by a woman. He carried on many of Kennedy's programs and was particularly effective at gaining legislation in civil rights and social programs. He was elected in his own right in 1964. During the mid-sixties the Vietnam War escalated and Johnson began to send troops and supplies to South Vietnam.

As the War intensified, he committed more troops and money. Domestic programs began to suffer and casualties from the war surpassed those suffered in Korea. Riots and unrest over the war broke out at home and Johnson's popularity plummeted. He did not run for reelection in 1968 but retired to his ranch where he died of a heart attack four years later.

Location: Family Cemetery, Stonewall, Texas, 14 miles west of Johnson City, Texas off U. S. Highway 290.

Burial Facts: Buried the farthest south, Johnson died of a heart attack at age 64. He is buried on his ranch in Stonewall Texas. Following the tradition started by his grandmother, Johnson is buried with his feet to the east, as was the custom of the Plains Indians. His wife Claudia (Lady Bird) Taylor Johnson still lives at the ranch.

Graveside Condition: Well-preserved and protected by National Parks personnel.

Directions: Midway between Fredericksburg, Texas and Johnson City, Texas on U. S. Highway 290 is the LBJ Ranch at Stonewall, Texas. Main entrance to Lyndon B. Johnson State Historical Park is on U. S. Highway 290. Trams from Visitors' Center transport visitors to gravesite across the Pedernalis River.

Richard M. Nixon
37th President 1969 - 1974

Richard Nixon (signature)

Born: Yorba Linda, California
January 9, 1913

Died: New York City, New York
April 22, 1994

Age at Death: 81

Place of Burial: Richard Nixon Library and Birthplace

Yorba Linda, California

CALIFORNIA

Richard Nixon Library and Birthplace

Born and buried the farthest west of any President, Richard Milhous Nixon holds the distinction of being the only Vice President to become President without immediately succeeding his predecessor after the predecessor left office, and the only President to resign from the Presidency.

President Nixon moved from Yorba Linda to Whittier, California when he was six years of age, where his father owned and operated a grocery store and gasoline station. After graduating from Whittier High School, he attended Whittier College and, upon graduation, was awarded a scholarship to attend Law School at Duke University. He returned to California to practice law and married Catherine "Pat" Ryan in 1940. When the United States entered World War II, Nixon obtained a commission as an officer in the U. S. Navy and served as an air transport officer in the Pacific Theater. He rose to the rank of Lieutenant Commander. After the war he ran for Congress, was elected, and served two terms in the House of Representatives. In 1950 he ran successfully for the U. S. Senate. In 1952 Nixon was selected by Dwight Eisenhower as his running mate and was elected Vice President under President Eisenhower. In 1960 he received the Republican nomination for President but lost to John F. Kennedy in one of the closest elections in this century. After an unsuccessful bid for the Governorship of California in 1962, he quit politics and returned to the practice of law. However, because of his work on behalf of Republican candidates around the United States, Nixon was nominated for President in 1968 narrowly defeating Hubert Humphrey, the Democratic candidate, and George Wallace, a third party candidate.

In his reelection of 1972 Nixon defeated his opponent by over 17.5 million popular votes which was the largest margin in the history of United States' elections. During the campaign, the office of the Democratic national headquarters in the Watergate complex in Washington D.C. was burglarized. After the burglars were apprehended, it was learned that members of Nixon's staff had first-hand knowledge of the crime. Nixon denied any knowledge of a cover-up of this incident, but an extensive investigation found that he did. After Congress began proceedings of impeachment, Nixon resigned on August 9, 1974. President Ford, succeeding Nixon to the Presidency, granted Nixon an unconditional pardon for any wrongdoings which he may have committed, thus Nixon was never prosecuted.

Even though he brought an end to the Vietnam war, opened productive talks and improved relations with China and the Soviet Union, and was also one of the most talented Presidents in Foreign Policy, his actions with regards to the Watergate scandal brought down his Presidency. After resigning, he was still sought by the Presidents who succeeded him to provide advice and service in the Foreign Policy arena where his expertise proved invaluable.

During his presidency, astronauts first landed on the moon, and he was the first President to visit China while in office. President Nixon ended the military draft in 1973, inititated the first attempts at a national health care plan, and negotiated the first definitive nuclear arms limitation treaty with the Soviet Union.

Up to the time of his death, Nixon was included in the largest number of living ex-Presidents in the twentieth century: Nixon, Ford, Carter, Reagan, and Bush.

From the death of Lyndon Johnson to Richard Nixon, over twenty years elapsed, making it the greatest expanse of time between the deaths of two Presidents.

President Nixon's gravestone reads:

The greatest honor history can bestow
Is the title of peacemaker.

Burial Facts: Richard Nixon died of complications four days after a stroke at age 81 in 1994. He is buried at the Richard M. Nixon Library and Birthplace in Yorba Linda, California, along with his wife, Thelma Catherine "Pat" Ryan, who died in 1993.

Graveside Condition: Excellent. Preserved and maintained by the Richard Nixon Library and Birthplace Foundation, a non-profit organization.

Directions: From State Highway 57, also known as the Orange Freeway, exit Yorba Linda Blvd. and travel east approximately 3 1/2 miles. The entrance to the Museum and Birthplace is approximately 1/2 block east of Eureka Blvd. on the North side of the street.

Western Tour

Richard M. Nixon - Yorba Linda, California
Lyndon Johnson - Stonewall, Texas
Dwight David Eisenhower - Abilene, Kansas
Harry S. Truman - Independence, Missouri

Midwestern Tour

Herbert Hoover - West Branch, Iowa
Abraham Lincoln - Springfield, Illinois
Benjamin Harrison - Indianapolis, Indiana
Zachary Taylor - Louisville, Kentucky
William H. Harrison - North Bend, Ohio
Warren Harding - Marion, Ohio
Rutherford Hayes - Fremont, Ohio
James Garfield - Cleveland, Ohio
William McKinley - Canton, Ohio

Southern Tour

James K. Polk - Nashville, Tennessee
Andrew Jackson - Nashville, Tennessee
Andrew Johnson - Greeneville, Tennessee
Thomas Jefferson - Charlottesville, Virginia
James Madison - Montpelier Station, Virginia
James Monroe - Richmond, Virginia
John Tyler - Richmond, Virginia
George Washington - Mt. Vernon, Virginia
William H. Taft - Arlington, Virginia
John Kennedy - Arlington, Virginia
Woodrow Wilson - Washington, D.C.

Eastern Tour

James Buchanan - Lancaster, Pennsylvania
Grover Cleveland - Princeton, New Jersey
U. S. Grant - New York City, New York
Theodore Roosevelt - Oyster Bay (Long Island), N.Y.
Franklin Roosevelt - Hyde Park, New York
John Adams and John Q. Adams - Quincy, Massachusetts
Franklin Pierce - Concord, New Hampshire
Calvin Coolidge - Plymouth, Vermont
Martin Van Buren - Kinderhook, New York
Chester Arthur - Albany, New York
Millard Fillmore - Buffalo, New York